# Everyday Miracles

Jenny Morelli

BookLeaf
Publishing

India | USA | UK

Made with ❤ on the BookLeaf Publishing Platform
www.bookleafpub.in
www.bookleafpub.com

# Dedication

To my hubby Mikey, my constant backyard companion who enjoys nature and our yard pets as much as I do. Thank you, also, to Nutty and his squirrel siblings, the four incredible deer, the raccoon, the chipmunk, bunny, blue jays, cardinals, grackles, super-grackles, and mourning doves who frequent my yard for the best peanuts and corn in all the land.

# Preface

# Acknowledgements

Thank you always to my number one fan, my husband Mikey, and my many students who've adopted me as their school mom. I'd also love to thank the amazing non-profit organization Project Write Now for reminding me how much I love to write and inspiring me to rekindle my love for words, with a special shoutout to Laura Cyphers, my poetry instructor. Thank you, also, to my faithful brother John and sister Lizzie for patiently reading everything I've ever written.

# 1. The Fawn

**The Fawn**
I shook the corn bin
let the corn rattle
so the fawns would hear
their cotton-soft satellite ears twitching
as they turned to me
as they backed up
as they let me approach the bowls
to fill them.
One retreated into the ivy,
wary and watching me
from a safer distance;
the other
stood her ground
stomped her hoof once
twice
thrice
sending small but powerful
earthquakes my way
in warning
or in acceptance.
I lowered myself to the ground
and she one-step
two-step...

came to me
nuzzled her wet licorice nose
into the bowl I held
and crunch-crunch-crunched
then raised her head,
her syrupy eyes locked on mine
and swallowed,
her throat moving as the corn passed through
and retreated one step
then another
allowing me
to rise
allowing me
to take one slow step
then another
until I was back inside
back behind the cat-scratched screen
back behind the rain-stained glass door
a newfound trust
as the fawn pranced off
on her stilt legs
into the night
ending our evening
dance.

# 2. Joy in the Ordinary

**Joy in the Ordinary**

I'm not quite sure
Where ordinary falls
On the squirrel spectrum,
But yesterday was a joyful day
In so many ways, and it all began
With my car's battery dying
Because I left my keys in the ignition
Overnight.
I beat myself up
For hours about missing
The first day of work after spring break
as my hubby
Walked down the road
And lugged back a new battery
And installed the damn thing
With our nosy neighbor's help,
While I prepared a feast for my outdoor
Wildlife creatures
Who I worried would be disoriented and confused
By the impending phenomenon
Mere hours away,
As predicted by the experts.
I filled bowls full of corn and peanuts

And water and by ten in the morning,
Hubby and I had settled into our lounge chairs
In our yard
under a perfectly splendid
Golden sun preparing to kiss the moon mid-day
And worked
on our first-of-the-season suntans,
And just when I thought the I-normally-hate
Mondays Monday
Couldn't get any better,
Nutty arrived,
Nose and tail twitching,
Up on his hind legs mere feet
From my feet,
As if to say 'Hey, Peanut Lady!
Care to share a nut or two?'
And so I brought out a cup
And sat cross-legged in my grass,
And proceeded to spend an hour or two
Feeding Nutty one peanut at a time
As if together we were welcoming this glorious spring
day
So welcome
After so much rain,
And when he ran off
To seek cover from the eclipse,
I headed inside to grab my glasses,

But the day of wonder didn't end there,
As, earlier than usual, my three neighborhood
Deer arrived to crunch the corn
From the overflowing bowls
I always leave out, and the bluejays
and grackles and cardinals and mourning doves
All flew to and fro as the moon floated off once more
And the world cranked back to normal
And I could finally breathe
A sigh of relief.
I'm not quite sure
Where ordinary falls
In my daily life,
But yesterday was a joyful day
In so many ways, and it all began
With my car's battery dying
Because I left my keys in the ignition
Overnight.

# 3. Surround Sounds

Faraway cars
zooming along the highway.
Bumper mewling her woeful loneliness.
Simba
is somewhere,
surely snoring. The crackle
of my coffee-scented candle. My breathing.
The voices in my mind,
right now
singing a song
*Hoods turned heroes*
about underdogs having their moment;
ideas swimming through the currents of the song
trying
to gain purchase
onto the dry land of this page.
If I were to open my window, the leaves
would be scurrying along crunchy autumn grass.
Fallen twigs and branches
would be clawing
at the ground. Nutty might be
cracking a shell and munching on peanuts.
The deer and her pups
might be crunching

on corn,
but alas, inside I remain,
windows closed against the chilly air,
and thoughts and snores and mewls are all I have
for symphony and company,
until reality
cranks
back to life
with Simba howling
and Bumper hissing and growling
and I join in
with the sounds
of my sighs and the skittering
of my fingers across the keyboard's keys
in perfect harmony.

# 5. Tiny Green Plants

Tiny green plants
filled with possibility, providing breath
love and life to all. It's how the world began
with one
tiny green plant
squeezing through a crack
in the earth
to meet the sun.
Did that fragile soul
know what it started?
Did she know
how important she was?
Did she know
what essence meant,
what curiosity and perseverance
were when she poked through the darkness
to find the light?
Did she know that she
would become the catalyst
for life on this rock of a planet,
that every living thing would rely on her
for oxygen, for wisdom?
So much
depends on a tiny

green plant as we rush
through our existence unaware
sometimes even galloping along
trampling
what made us.
Is ignorance equal
to ingratitude? There's a reason
we should take time
to smell the flowers, to
acknowledge what came before us,
what created us through so much evolution.
As a living soul that spins in this crazy self-centered
world,
I wish
each of us
would take a moment
each day to stop and look around,
to listen to the birds and squirrels, the trees
and bees.
Maybe we'd hear
their unanswered *Where*
*have you been?* in their chirps
and barks and rustlings and buzzings,
and if we're really honest
with ourselves,
we'd admit...
There's nowhere else

I want to be. So thank you,
tiny green plant, for breath, for love,
for life
for possibility.
I lean into the rhythm
of your
heart.

# 6. Roots

I lack the peace
of simple things and wish for
the dumb life of roots, which may not be so dumb
after all, as they carry the essence
of life
in its simplest, purest form
without the concern for its next meal, without
the concern for survival
at all. No,
it does not lack the simple peace
we've lost
in our humanity and that is where
our truest roots lie...
in our plants herbs flowers earth
in our ancestors far back
before this free nation was claimed. No.
Do not mistake simple
pure or dumb
for weakness or ignorance. Roots
are wise enough to carry on
to sustain
and survive despite the complicated world
under which they live, despite

the world,
they will outlive.

# 7. The Oversized Orange

I just wasn't ready to be picked
I was enjoying
the sunshine too much;
I liked being kissed by its beams
cradled
by my tree's branches
protected by its leaves. I just
wasn't ready
to be plucked, and so
I ducked and hid and made
no eye contact
until I grew too big
until I met the three humans
who marveled at my beauty and size
I just
wasn't ready
to be picked until
I met them, felt their gentle smiles,
their soft hands
cradle and pluck and so
I gave myself to them to share
knowing this peace and contentment.
It's new.
I love you, Sun

and Tree and Humans.
I'm glad I exist.

15

# 8. Bumblebee

Kneeling on the edge of my garden box
classical music humming softly in my ears,
the early sun kisses my cheek as I slap at blood-thirsty
mosquitos.
I pluck mint leaves and drop them into a silver bowl
until my fingertip warms and burns like lava.

I panic as I spot your iridescent black-yellow fur cradled
in a large mint leaf.
I jump I stand I scramble back three steps, but you're not
moving.
Are you hurt? Did I kill you?
I must've pinched you. Please don't be dead.
I sit and study you as my finger swells, beg you to be
okay.
Please move. Please please please.

I wait and hope as the sun shifts and my skin roasts and
my shadow lengthens.
And then it happens. In the orangey glow of dusk,
your leg twitches under your shiny coat. The others
unfurl, tentative, cautious.
Your wings spread and you lift into the air, testing your
equipment

You float and hover and linger before me like Tinkerbell
and I hold my breath.

I whisper *Can you forgive me?* and you pause as if
considering
then bumble your dizzy flight back into my minty
world.
I exhale my gratitude that I only spooked you,
That your precious life is intact, though mine is changed
forever.

# 9. Acorns and Squirrels

Yesterday,
I sat with a book
to read one fun thing. But then
an acorn fell like spare change followed closely
by a squirrel, cautious,
hesitant
weighing his options, weighing
his risk-reward dilemma.
He did not
dance
as squirrels are apt to do,
but instead shifted
slowly
deliberately
from one paw to another
a perfect example of the many kinds
of people in our
world
with the same internal
struggles; those who have and those
who have not and I wondered which one this squirrel
might be.
Was he adding
to his yard booty, or lost

alone and bereft? I let myself feel myself
the way that squirrel might
if he risked
traversing me
for the nut held snug
in the pages of my book before,
with great thoughtfulness, placing the acorn
onto the ground.
His curiosity
turned to confusion
before he turned and scampered off
into the ivy and after scoffing at his judgment, his
stupidity for rejecting free food,
I thought maybe
we're all
a little mixed up.

# 10. A Simple Moment

Hours before sunrise
and not fully awake
I pulled open
the door,
slid open
the screen
came face to face
with the baby deer
hours before sunrise
half a day early,
her satellite ears
flicking back,
then toward me
as if to say
*Any breakfast corn*
*to spare?*
I stood still
to not startle the fawn,
and then
it dawned on me
just before this dawn
that maybe
she's staying still
so as not to startle me,

and so I approached
one step at a time
I lowered myself enough
to fill the bowls,
then retreated
to the patio
and watched her feast
as her brother and momma
joined her.

# 11. The Death of a Tree

The sound
of industrial machines
in a quiet residential neighborhood
too early in the morning can only be the sound
of a life
about to end.
And like a train wreck,
or a dying relative I suffer the compulsion
to hold a vigil to watch
to be
with that life
in its final moments.
What you don't know until you
own a home is that you're buying the beauty
and fragility
of all the lives that come
with the property; lives that were there
long before
you
wanted to rip it
from its roots to remove
some shade from your yard, or maybe
that magnificent tree was in the way of the pool
you wanted to install.

Taking care
and being aware
of life that helps us live
and breathe; is the simplest of human
gestures. Trees were here long before we were
and tearing them down
in their majestic
prime
is an atrocity
that's hard to witness.
But someone needs to absorb its pain
and so I sat in my yard today until the last
of that poor tree
was ripped and chipped
from my neighbor's yard. Are those
the sounds
the tree's anguish?
And in the gaping opening
left behind
the sun shines down on me
a simple solar solace, offering gratitude,
maybe,
or just a simple
Understanding and natural
reverence and comfort and companionship
universal to us
all.

# 14. What the Cats Know

A new beast
has arrived, threatening
my domain. She's pathetically,
shamelessly,
vomitously,
hairball-inducingly
cute.
She'll have to go,
that much is clear, but I don't know
how,
so here I sit,
outside her room
waiting for the human
to open the door.
Until then, I'll have myself
a little
nap,
simmering
and sleuthing;
listening and waiting...
Her thoughts wake me.
They drift to me
on rain's breath,
seducing, beckoning,

tempting and taunting.
This won't be over
until that wretched beast
is gone.
I know she knows something.
She can cute herself up all she likes,
but cats know stuff, it's our job, and two of us
in the same house
knowing
just will not do,
so while she's spending her days
outcuting herself,
I will spend mine
plotting.

# 16. Gardens for Sulking

Gardens
are also good places to sulk,
I've learned. There's nothing more rewarding
when I'm in a bad mood
than sitting
cross-legged in a box
of fertile soil and letting the spring sun
warm my worried mind
while I rip
and tear mint leaves
then lavender then lemon and basil,
inhaling their mixed fragrances and letting myself
remember
how intoxicating,
how medicinal such simple
scents of nature can be to clear away
my clouds,
and I've noticed
the same rules apply for other
living beings. I've commiserated
with a whole family of daddy long-legs
and also a bundle
of bumblebees, one in particular
who spent the day sulking with me when I accidentally

pinched it
while picking my leaves
because it was perched on the underside
of a large spearmint leaf for maybe some shaded refuge
from the sun.
That day, we sat for hours,
me, hoping the poor little thing was okay
and she,
keeping her five eyes on me
while taking the time to heal her wound
while I cooed
and apologized for hurting her;
yes, gardens are good places to sit and stew and sulk
until the sunshine
has pierced through the wrongs
I'm feeling so that she may shed light
on my darkest
concerns and remind me
that beauty, if given the chance
and the time, can lift even the heaviest of emotions.

# 1. Nature's Remedy

In my darkest moments
mid-night
when what I've poured
onto the page taunts me, I drown
in doubt that I'll never be
good enough.
But then
I rise
in the slant of morning
sunrise that slices through my snoring cat
and I breathe in, breathe out
and step outside,
remember
what's really important.
I throw peanuts to the squirrels
and birds. I water my new-bloomed
perennials.
I
inhale the scents
of unfurling mint and lemon
and lavender. It's nature's intervention,
a collective collaboration and meditation, a chance
to recalibrate
my miserable mood,

to remind myself that if I
can nurture
nature
I can surely cultivate
my own damn confidence.
I breathe in
the most joyous breath,
then breathe out a butterfly sigh,
and the softest, most powerful wish to pass along
an incantation
that will flit and flutter
to someone else in need of bliss
and respite from their woes. Breathe in,
breathe out. Spread light across the darkness. One life,
one breath, one sigh
at a time.

# 18. I Know Cats

I'd like to believe
I know a lot about cats. I know
they have three eyelids and their tongues
flip under to scoop in
water.
I know
that they are the perfect
killing machine; that when they roll
onto their backs, it's not
for a belly rub,
but instead
to prepare for murder,
their weapons releasing in a blink.
I know
that their purr
isn't always for pleasure,
but sometimes for pain and their slow
blink, blink, blinks
are little cat
kisses.
Yes,
I know a lot
about cats, but only
what they want me to know.

I also know
without a doubt that in their most content,
most contemplative moments,
they are communicating
through
their whiskers
and satellite ears with aliens
or gods or some other unknown entity
that knows
answers to questions
they've spent their lives pondering;
answers like
what their true name is
and when the world as we know it
will end
and though they have
no thumbs, they hold their cards
close and have the best
poker faces.
Blink.
Yawn.
Mic drop, Human.

# 19. The Thing in My Office

There's a small thing
flying around my office, invisible
to my naked eye, but quite there all the same,
somewhere deep within
my mind
and soul, just flitting about
like a sun-blinded bat; just buzzing about
like a hungry mosquito,
there,
but not quite,
and begging to be seen, to be
acknowledged
or even just noticed.
I can't give it the satisfaction,
just in case it is my doubt or my anxiety,
my anger, my sadness, my
emptiness;
can't give it even
the merest of glances lest it
dive-bomb me into a paralysis I just don't
have time for,
not right now or later
or tomorrow or ever. So here I sit,
staring at the computer screen, trying not to look,

not to look... not

to look

as it stares at me,

laser-focused and determined to derail me,

to distract me to defeat my resolve

and I just...

can't...

let it win; here I sit,

so curious...so curious...so curious

to take

just a peek,

in the hopes that it's something

I shouldn't lose like my phone, my wallet,

my keys,

and not something

I cannot, like my mind, my heart,

my soul, my

hope.

# 21. Divine Intervention

I can't sit
with myself. Can't meditate
worth a damn because of the incessant
busy-bee buzzing inside
my brain.
The more I try
to focus, the more distracts me,
like the student I overheard tell his classmate
his birthday's next Tuesday
but it's okay
if no one remembers. This
spins me into a spiral of dark thoughts
of a teen forgotten who's slid into his own dark place
and doesn't resurface,

or the blue jay
who's just landed on my chair,
who's watching my cat chomp a large
juicy spider,
head cocked and curious,
or the leaf-like bug making its turtle-slow
ascent
up my screen
or the squirrel who's just crept up and,

with front paws tucked
into his white-
bibbed
chest, is imploring me,
like orphan Oliver might, as if to ask
*Please, Sir, might you have some peanuts to spare?*
complete with British accent
if I had my druthers.
I've tried

blanking my mind. I've tried
yelling at myself *How many times do I have to tell you*
*to focus on more immediate*
*concerns*
*instead of reading,*
*eyes glazed over with words,*
*neglected spines of books wedged into bookcases,*
*the air crackling with guilt*
*and longing?*
That,
to me, is the most
divine of interventions, alluring, seductive,
begging for me to escape
for just a moment,
into another
world.

There are days
I just crash against
the not-knowingness of it all
and want to stay home, pet my cat, but alas,
I must work hard
to get out of my own way
and let it roll, this pent-up frustration.
Then,
there are days, or just moments
within the day, where I get that feeling of
okayness.
It's as endless
as a circle, these feelings
day by day, and when I can immerse myself
in one or more of my other worlds,
one which includes
my aunt
who took her own life,
I must pause and think who's to say
suicide is wrong

for someone who's just lost
the only life she knew? That is when the mystery
of a single line of poetry
unmoors me.
These,
I guess, are the notes of age

that can only happen with time and tide
and too much
pain,
and I want to take a break
to watch the big ball of fire in the sky rise and set
and rise again while I study
the fleeting dandelion
fluff.
I love those yellow globes,
and know that lovers are here; and know
that when I return to reality,
each rock,
sturdy
beneath my steps, will hold me
lead me, bring me
home.

But then, it all turns
Sideways when Simba vomits
the barely digested arachnid and the blue jay
poops
on the arm of my chair
and the squirrel starts a growling brawl
with his interloper twin and all I can think as I witness
this madness
is leave it to nature's divine
intervention to remind me of what really counts.

This
is where I find Divine in my poems,
or maybe where she
finds me.

# 22. The Illusive Idea

Catch an idea by her tail
before she flits away to someone else
someone willing
to capture her,
to trap her
between the blue bars
of a loose-leaf page, committed
and tamed, displayed like a
fall leaf
melted with crayons
and flattened between sheets
of wax paper and hung to glow in the sun
to be bleached into transparency.
Yes. Yes!
*That*


is what it feels like
to catch an idea by her tail, to wrangle her,
to write her into submission.
Such a savage, barbaric
victory
that leaves me ink-bloodied
and thought-drained, an utterly empty
pool. Yes. Yes!

*That*

is what happens when I'm focused enough
and driven enough, aware
and inspired and
creative enough to grab an idea
as she flutters by, as she
buzzes by

to catch as she weaves
through the mint in my mind. Who knows!
She might become
a bumblefly
or a butterbee or whatever else
my mind can grow
in its garden.

# 23. This Poem Is a Dream

You
are a field
as long as flowers and fireflies
float and flit in your space, as long as spiders
spin their webs of wonder
in your valleys.
You're a field
as long as the earth spins
and the sun shines
and the moon glows
and the stars fall
and flowers flourish.
You are a field
because it takes a long time
to see and hear and feel,
to taste and smell the truths of this world
that may spark more than six senses in the end.
You are a field
until our love language
catches up to us.
I know
we are still adjusting
to our distance and permanence
through time and space, but shortcuts

and landmarks
are everywhere
if only
we know ourselves enough
and trust ourselves enough to find them.
This poem is a dream
telling you that you are a field
and I am your firefly
flower.

# 24. The Masked Bandit

At four o'clock,
it's dark and my body
is succumbing to the night shivers
of sleepiness,
of day's over, of
try again tomorrow
because that is what New Jersey's doing
on this late autumn evening as frost falls like feathers
onto the grass blades'
tips
and smothers
the car's windshield
and Simba has settled into
the very center of our new plush blanket
for his fifth or tenth
winter's nap
today.

At four o'clock,
it's dark and my world
is shutting down so that I
may share the sunshine with others
who've been waiting while my eyelids droop
and my breathing

slows
and I huddle
into myself and I grow
heavier sleepier and snorier
and succumb to the night to recharge
so that I may try again
tomorrow
and that's when I hear it
the scritch scritch scritch in the kitchen.
I get up, glancing for Simba nestled in by my side
and tiptoe into the kitchen, where I find, on the other
side
of my sliding glass door
a huge
and furry masked bandit
hanging from the screen staring at me,
glaring at me, *imploring me?* before carefully
climbing back down, down, down, one raccoon paw
at a time, his eyes
never leaving mine until
he's reached the ground, and then
he lumbers off into the darkness once more,
Leaving me
To wonder, as I shuffled
back to my bedroom, why was he here
and what did he want, and how on earth did he climb
so high

and what was he
searching for or climbing toward?
My body
was buzzing
after such adventures,
mind humming with too many
questions to settle back in to a proper night's
snooze.

50

# 26. We Can, Too

My heart
has been lead
these last few days,
a heavy, weighted thing
sinking into the abyss, but then,
as if thrust from the darkness, a new deer
appeared,
shuffling through my ivy
to remind me of the beauty that remains
indifferent of all human-tethered concerns,
and suddenly,
my heart was floating
like the errant firefly among
the dusky shadows, was fluttering
like the cardinals
and blue jays in all their brilliant
colors alighting on my peanut-filled grill,
was flitting to and fro
like the squirrels on my tree,
was singing nature's songs as if
to let me know that as long as earth's beauty
can weather whatever storms are thrown its way,
then hope remains

that we can,
too.

# 27. The World Goes On

There's an undercurrent
of unease pulsing
just beneath this country.
Lines are drawn.
Bonds have been severed.
So much divide
to our united,
but then, satellite ears twitch
flick toward my movement;
stilt legs falter
just beyond the floodlight,
head lowering again
upon sensing I'm safe,
upon sensing I'm there
to refill her bowl, a comfort
in these trying times.
Such unease
pulsing just beneath us.
Lines drawn. Bonds
severed; meanwhile,
the world goes on.

9 789367 213818 4